This workbook is dedicated to the dreamers, innovators, and entrepreneurs who dare to build brands that inspire and endure. Here's to your journey of building a legacy, one trademark at a time.

by :

THE LAW FIRM OF
ANDREA HENCE EVANS
PATENT · TRADEMARK · COPYRIGHT

INVEST IN YOUR IDEA®

Contact Information

www.evansiplaw.com

Office (301) 497-9997

info@evansiplaw.com

Table of Contents

Introduction to Trademarks

What is a Trademark?

A trademark is a type of intellectual property that serves as a recognizable sign, design, or expression identifying products or services from a particular source. Trademarks are crucial for brand identity and play a significant role in consumer protection and fair competition in the marketplace.

Types of Trademarks

- **Word Marks:** These consist of words, letters, numbers, or any combination thereof. Examples include "Coca-Cola" or "IBM."

- **Design Marks:** These are graphical elements, symbols, or logos. The Nike swoosh is a famous example.

- **Slogans:** Phrases used to identify and distinguish a brand, such as McDonald's "I'm lovin' it."

- **Trade Dress:** The overall commercial image of a product, which may include its packaging, color, or design. The distinctive shape of a Coca-Cola bottle is an example of trade dress.

- **Sound Marks:** Unique sounds that identify a brand, like the NBC chimes or the MGM lion's roar.

- **Color Marks:** In some cases, a specific color used in a particular way can be trademarked, such as Tiffany Blue.

- **Scent Marks:** Although rare, distinctive scents can sometimes be trademarked, like the scent of Play-Doh.

Interactive Element

Can you think of an example for each type of trademark listed above?

Write them down:

- Word Mark: _____
- Design Mark:_____
- Slogan: _____
- Trade Dress: _____
- Sound Mark: _____
- Color Mark: _____
- Scent Mark: _____

The Difference Between TM and ®

As shown in the graphic, there's an important distinction between the TM (™) and ® symbols often seen with trademarks:

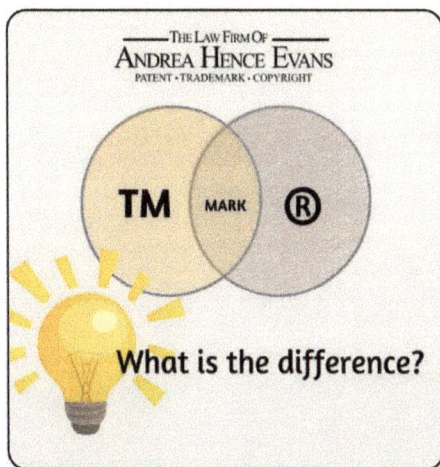

THE LAW FIRM OF
ANDREA HENCE EVANS
PATENT · TRADEMARK · COPYRIGHT

TM   MARK   ®

What is the difference?

TM (™) Symbol	® Symbol
• The TM symbol indicates that a mark is being used as a trademark, but it has not been registered with the United States Patent and Trademark Office (USPTO). • It can be used with any mark that a business wishes to claim as its trademark. • It provides no legal protection, but it serves as a public notice of the owner's claim to the mark.	• The ® symbol indicates that a trademark has been registered with the USPTO. • It can only be used after the USPTO has granted registration. • Using this symbol with an unregistered mark is against the law.

The "Mark" in the Middle

The overlapping area in the Venn diagram represents the mark itself - the word, logo, or other identifier that is being used as a trademark. Whether it's designated with TM or ®, the underlying mark remains the same; what changes is its legal status and the protections it enjoys.

Interactive Element

Look at five products or advertisements around you. How many use the TM symbol? How many use the ® symbol? List them here:

TM symbols:

1. _____
2. _____
3. _____
4. _____
5. _____

® symbols:

1. _____
2. _____
3. _____
4. _____
5. _____

Why are Trademarks Important?

Trademarks serve several crucial functions in commerce:

- **Source Identification:** They help consumers identify the source of goods or services.
- **Quality Assurance:** Trademarks often carry with them an implied level of quality, based on consumers' past experiences with the brand.
- **Advertising and Marketing:** A strong trademark can become a valuable asset in marketing campaigns.
- **Asset Value:** Well-established trademarks can become extremely valuable corporate assets.
- **Legal Protection:** Registered trademarks provide legal recourse against infringement.
- **Brand Loyalty:** Trademarks help build and maintain customer loyalty.
- **Competitive Advantage:** A strong trademark can differentiate a business from its competitors.

The Scope of Trademark Protection

It's important to understand that trademark rights are:

- **Territorial:** Rights are generally limited to the country where the mark is registered or used.
- **Industry-Specific:** Protection typically extends only to the specific goods or services for which the mark is registered or used.
- **Use-Based:** In many countries, including the U.S., trademark rights stem from actual use of the mark in commerce.
- **Time-Limited:** While trademark rights can theoretically last forever, they require periodic renewal and continued use.
- **Strength-Dependent**: The level of protection a trademark receives often depends on its distinctiveness or "strength."

Interactive Element

Think of a business you'd like to start. What would be your ideal trademark, and why? How might it serve the functions we discussed above?

Your Business Idea: _____

Proposed Trademark: _____

How it serves trademark functions:

_____
_____
_____
_____
_____
_____
_____

Trademarks vs. Other Forms of Intellectual Property

To fully understand trademarks, it's helpful to compare them to other forms of intellectual property:

- **Patents:** Protect inventions and discoveries.
  - Duration: Generally 20 years from filing date.
  - Example: The unique mechanism inside a new type of can opener.

- **Copyrights:** Protect original works of authorship.
  - Duration: Life of the author plus 70 years (for individual works).
  - Example: The text of a novel or the code of a software program.

- **Trade Secrets:** Protect confidential business information.
  - Duration: As long as the information remains secret.
  - Example: The recipe for Coca-Cola.

The Importance of Trademark Searches

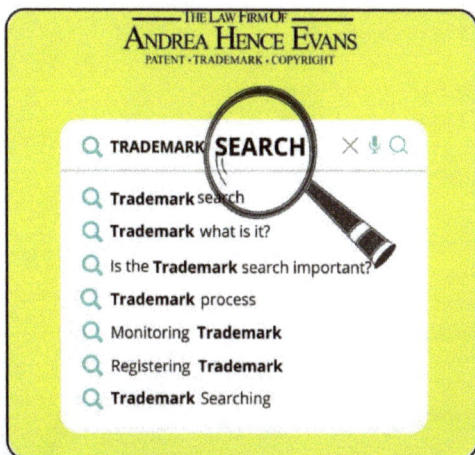

Why Conduct a Trademark Search?

As shown in the graphic, there are several key reasons why conducting a trademark search is crucial:

- **Avoiding Conflicts:** To ensure your proposed mark doesn't conflict with existing trademarks.
- **Understanding the Landscape:** To gain insights into similar marks in your industry.
- **Saving Time and Money:** To prevent investing in a mark that may not be available for use or registration.
- **Strategic Decision-Making:** To make informed decisions about your branding strategy.
- **Identifying Potential Opposition:** To anticipate and prepare for possible challenges to your application.
- **Assessing Mark Strength:** To understand how distinctive your mark is in the marketplace.

Types of Trademark Searches

1. Preliminary (Knockout) Search: A quick search to identify any obvious conflicts.
- Pros: Fast, cost-effective
- Cons: May miss less obvious conflicts

2. Comprehensive Search: A thorough search of federal and state registrations, common law uses, and domain names.
- Pros: Provides a detailed picture of the trademark landscape
- Cons: More time-consuming and expensive

3. International Search: If you plan to use your mark internationally, searching in relevant countries is crucial.
- Pros: Essential for global brand protection
- Cons: Can be complex due to differing laws and language barriers

4. Industry-Specific Search: Focuses on trademarks within your particular industry or product category.
- Pros: Helps identify the most relevant potential conflicts
- Cons: May miss conflicts with marks in related industries

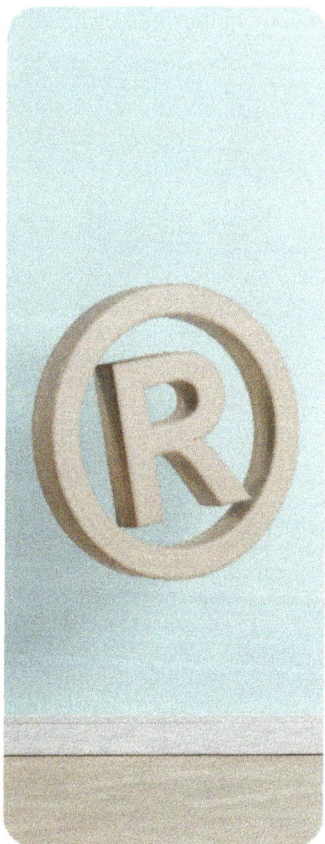

Why Conduct a Trademark Search?

Using USPTO.gov to Search

- Go to USPTO website (www.uspto.gov)
- Navigate the field of the search
  - Wordmark
  - Goods & Services
  - Owner
  - Serial Number
  - Registration Number
  - Mark Description
  - Design Code
  - Design Description
  - Field Tag and Search Builder
- Enter your search terms
- Review the results carefully

Interactive Element

Using USPTO.gov, perform a basic word mark search for your proposed trademark from the previous exercise. What did you find? Were there any similar marks?

Search Results: _____

Similar Marks Found: _____

Advanced Search Strategies

1. **Use of Wildcards:** Employ "" to replace any number of characters, or "?" to replace a single character. Example: "cat" would find "cat," "cats," "catch," etc.

2. **Design Code Searching:** For logo marks, use the USPTO's design code manual to search for similar designs.

3. **Owner Searching:** Search for other marks owned by your competitors.

4. **Class Searching**: Look for marks in the same or related international classes as your goods/services.

Interpreting Search Results

When reviewing search results, consider:

- Similarity in appearance, sound, or meaning
- Relatedness of goods or services
- Strength of the existing mark
- Evidence of actual confusion
- Channels of trade
- Type of consumers and degree of consumer care

What if You Find a Similar Mark?

If you find a similar mark, you have several options:

- Abandon your proposed mark and choose a new one
- Modify your mark to make it more distinctive
- Limit your goods/services to avoid overlap
- Consider coexistence strategies, such as consent agreements
- Proceed with your application, prepared to argue against a likelihood of confusion

The Risks of Not Conducting a Proper Search

Failing to conduct a thorough trademark search can lead to several risks:

- **Infringement Liability:** You could be sued for trademark infringement.
- **Wasted Resources:** Money spent on branding and marketing could be lost.
- **Forced Rebranding:** You may have to change your brand after establishing it in the market.
- **Reputation Damage:** Your business could be seen as careless or unethical.

Interactive Element

Based on your search results, do you need to modify your proposed trademark? If so, how?

Modified Trademark: _____

Reason for Modification: _____

The USPTO Trademark Registration Process

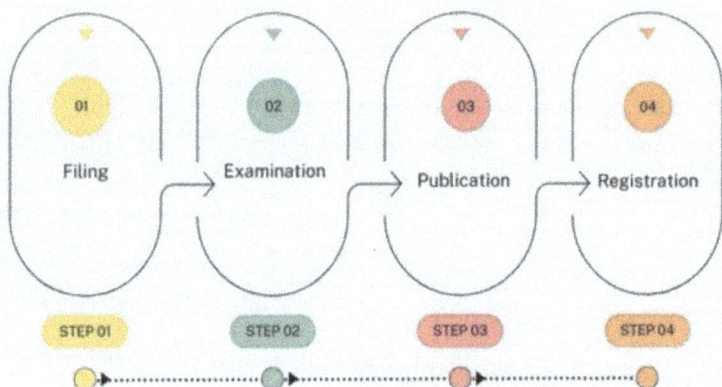

THE LAW FIRM OF

ANDREA HENCE EVANS

PATENT · TRADEMARK · COPYRIGHT

The USPTO Trademark Timeline

01	02	03	04
Filing	Examination	Publication	Registration
STEP 01	STEP 02	STEP 03	STEP 04

The USPTO trademark registration process consists of four main steps, as illustrated in the timeline graphic from The Law Firm of Andrea Hence Evans. Let's explore each step in detail:

Step 01: Filing

The first step in the trademark registration process is filing your application with the USPTO.

Key aspects of this step include:

- Preparing your application, including identifying your mark and listing your goods/services
- Choosing your filing basis (use in commerce or intent to use)
- Submitting your application through the Trademark Electronic Application System (TEAS)
- Paying the required filing fee

Interpreting Search Results

Before filing, you should:

- ☐ Conduct a comprehensive trademark search
- ☐ Determine your filing basis
- ☐ Identify your mark format (standard character, stylized/design, or sound mark)
- ☐ Prepare a clear description of your goods or services
- ☐ Gather specimens of use (if applicable)
- ☐ Determine your filing fee

Components of a Trademark Application

A complete trademark application includes:

- ☐ Owner Information: Legal name and address of the trademark owner
- ☐ Contact Information: For correspondence with the USPTO
- ☐ The Mark: A clear depiction of your trademark
- ☐ Goods and Services: A specific description of what your mark represents
- ☐ Filing Basis: Either "use in commerce" or "intent to use"
- ☐ Specimen: For "use in commerce" applications
- ☐ Filing Fee: Varies based on the type of application

Interactive Element

What information do you think you need to gather before filing a trademark application?

_____
_____
_____
_____
_____
_____
_____
_____
_____

Step 02: Examination

Once your application is filed, it moves to the examination phase.

During this step:
- The USPTO assigns an examining attorney to your application
- The attorney reviews your application for compliance with legal requirements
- If issues are found, the attorney issues an Office Action
- You must respond to any Office Actions within six months

What Examiners Look For

- Likelihood of confusion with existing marks
- Distinctiveness of the mark
- Descriptiveness or genericness
- Proper specimen of use (for in-use applications)
- Accuracy and completeness of the application

Office Actions

If issues are found, the examiner will issue an Office Action, which:
- Explains any refusals to register the mark
- Details any requirements or requests for additional information
- Provides a deadline for response (typically 6 months)

Types of refusals include:
- Likelihood of confusion
- Descriptiveness
- Genericness
- Geographical descriptiveness
- Surname refusal

Responding to Office Actions

When responding to an Office Action:

- Address each issue raised by the examiner
- Provide evidence or legal arguments to support your position
- Meet the deadline (or request an extension if needed)
- Consider seeking legal assistance for complex issues

Interactive Element

What are some potential issues an examining attorney might find in a trademark application?

_____

_____

_____

_____

_____

_____

_____

Publication

Step 03: Publication

If your application passes the examination phase, it moves to publication.

This step involves:
- Your mark being published in the Official Gazette, the USPTO's weekly publication
- A 30-day opposition period where third parties can object to your registration
- If no opposition is filed, your application moves to the next step

The Opposition Process

If someone believes they would be harmed by the registration of your mark, they can file an opposition. This process involves:

- Filing a Notice of Opposition
- Presenting evidence and arguments before the Trademark Trial and Appeal Board (TTAB)
- Receiving a decision from the TTAB

Responding to Office Actions

In some cases, similar marks may coexist through a concurrent use proceeding, which allows registration of similar marks if:

- The marks have been used concurrently for some time
- No likelihood of confusion exists due to distinct geographic areas of use

Interactive Element
Why do you think there's a publication phase in the trademark registration process?

Your thoughts: _____

_____

Step 04: Registration

The final step in the process is registration.

At this stage:
- If no opposition was filed (or you overcame any oppositions), your mark is registered
- You receive a certificate of registration from the USPTO
- Your mark is added to the USPTO's database of registered trademarks

Rights Conferred by Registration

Federal registration provides several benefits:

- Nationwide priority (as of the filing date)
- Use of the ® symbol
- Listing in the USPTO database
- Basis for international registration
- Ability to record the registration with U.S. Customs to prevent importation of infringing goods
- Prima facie evidence of the mark's validity and your exclusive right to use it

Post-Registration Responsibilities

Registration is not the end of your trademark journey. To maintain your rights, you must:

- Use the mark consistently in commerce
- Monitor for potential infringement
- File required maintenance documents

Interactive Element

Once your trademark is registered, what do you think are your responsibilities as a trademark owner?

_____
_____
_____
_____
_____
_____
_____
_____
_____
_____
_____

Timeline Considerations

As shown in the graphic, the trademark registration process follows a linear path from filing to registration. However, it's important to note that:

- The time between each step can vary significantly depending on various factors.
- If issues arise during examination or if an opposition is filed, the process may take longer.
- Some applications may not make it all the way to registration if they don't overcome objections or oppositions.

> ### *Interactive Element*
> Based on what you've learned, estimate how long you think each step might take:
>
> - Filing to Examination: _____
> - Examination to Publication: _____
> - Publication to Registration: _____

Understanding this timeline is crucial for managing expectations and planning your branding strategy. Remember, while you can use your mark before registration (with the ™ symbol), the ® symbol can only be used after successful registration.

The Role of Attorneys in Trademark Registration

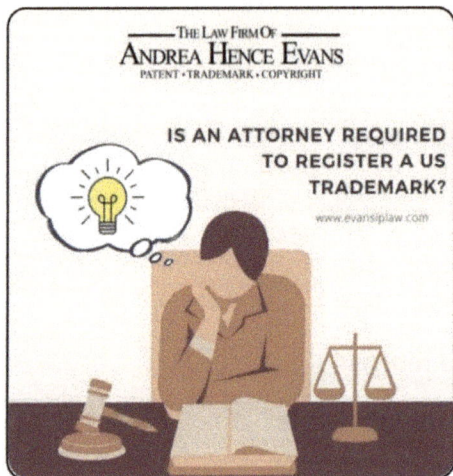

Do You Need an Attorney?

While it's not legally required to have an attorney to register a trademark, there are several reasons why it might be beneficial:

- **Expertise:** Trademark attorneys understand the intricacies of trademark law and USPTO procedures.
- **Improved Odds**: Applications filed by attorneys tend to have a higher success rate.
- **Time-Saving:** An attorney can handle the details, freeing you to focus on your business.
- **Strategic Advice:** Attorneys can provide valuable insights on trademark selection and protection strategies.
- **Navigating Complexity:** For complex applications or if issues arise, an attorney's expertise can be crucial.

When an Attorney is Particularly Helpful

- **Complex Applications:** If your application involves unusual goods/services or legal issues.
- **Office Actions:** If you receive an Office Action, especially one raising substantive issues.
- **Opposition Proceedings:** If someone opposes your application, legal representation is crucial.
- **International Protection:** If you're seeking trademark protection in multiple countries.
- **Enforcement:** When you need to defend your mark against infringement or challenge someone else's mark.

What to Expect When Working with a Trademark Attorney

- **Initial Consultation:** Discuss your business, proposed mark, and goals.
- **Comprehensive Search:** A thorough search for potential conflicts.
- **Application Preparation:** Drafting and filing your application.
- **Ongoing Communication:** Updates on your application's progress.
- **Office Action Responses:** If needed, preparing and filing responses.
- **Post-Registration Advice:** Guidance on using and maintaining your mark.

Costs of Hiring an Attorney

While hiring an attorney involves additional costs, it's important to weigh these against the potential benefits:

- Initial consultations are often free or low-cost
- Search and application fees typically range from $500 to $2,000
- Responding to Office Actions or handling oppositions can incur additional fees
- Complex cases or litigation can be significantly more expensive

Remember, these costs are in addition to USPTO filing fees.

Alternatives to Hiring an Attorney

If you decide not to hire an attorney, consider these alternatives:

- **USPTO Resources:** The USPTO website offers extensive guidance for applicants.
- **TEAS Plus:** This streamlined application process offers lower fees but has stricter requirements.
- **Trademark Legal Clinics:** Some law schools offer free trademark services to eligible individuals and small businesses.
- **Online Legal Services:** Some websites offer trademark registration services at lower costs than traditional attorneys.

Remember, while these options may save money upfront, they may not provide the same level of expertise and personalized guidance as a trademark attorney.

Trademark Monitoring and Maintenance

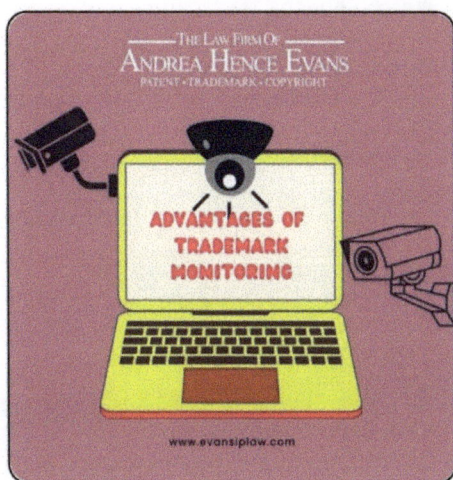

Why Monitor Your Trademark?

As illustrated in the graphic, there are several key advantages to trademark monitoring:

- **Early Detection:** Identify potential infringement early.
- **Brand Protection:** Safeguard your brand's reputation and distinctiveness.
- **Enforce Rights:** Take timely action against unauthorized use.
- **Market Intelligence:** Stay informed about competitor activities.
- **Maintain Trademark Strength:** Consistent enforcement helps maintain the strength of your mark.
- **Prevent Genericide:** Ensure your mark doesn't become generic through improper use

How to Monitor Your Trademark

The Law Firm of Andrea Hence Evans, LLC offers trademark monitoring services.

- **Set Up Google Alerts:** For your mark and variations.
- **Use Trademark Watch Services:** Professional services that monitor new applications and registrations.
- **Monitor Social Media:** Look for unauthorized use on various platforms.
- **Regularly Search Online Marketplaces:** Check for counterfeit goods or unauthorized use.
- **Domain Name Monitoring:** Watch for similar domain name registrations.
- **Industry Publications:** Keep an eye on trade journals and industry news.

Trademark Maintenance Requirements

- **Between 5th and 6th Year:** File a Declaration of Use (Section 8 Affidavit)
- **Between 9th and 10th Year**: File a Combined Declaration of Use and Application for Renewal (Sections 8 and 9)
- **Every 10 Years Thereafter:** Continue to file Combined Declarations/Renewals

Section 8 Declaration

This document affirms that your mark is still in use in commerce. You must provide:

- A statement that the mark is in use in commerce
- The date of first use of the mark in commerce
- Specimens showing how the mark is currently used

Section 9 Renewal

This document renews your registration for an additional 10-year period. It's typically combined with the Section 8 Declaration after the first 10-year period.

Proper Trademark Use

To maintain the strength of your mark:

- Use it consistently: Don't alter the appearance or wording of your mark.
- Use it as an adjective, not a noun or verb: Say "KLEENEX tissues," not just "KLEENEX."
- Distinguish it from surrounding text: Use all caps, bold, italics, or "quotation marks."
- Use the appropriate symbol: ™ for unregistered marks, ® for registered marks.
- Develop brand guidelines: Ensure all employees and partners use the mark correctly.

Consequences of Improper Trademark Maintenance

Failing to properly maintain your trademark can lead to:

- Loss of registration
- Weakening of trademark rights
- Difficulty enforcing your mark against infringers
- Potential genericide of your mark

Interactive Element

Create a 10-year trademark maintenance plan for your mark:

Year 1 (Registration): _____

Year 5-6: _____

Year 9-10: _____

Ongoing Monitoring Plan: _____

Common Trademark Issues and How to Avoid Them

Descriptiveness	• **Issue:** Marks that merely describe characteristics of the goods/services are weak and difficult to register. Solution: Choose suggestive, arbitrary, or fanciful marks instead. **Example:** "Speedy Auto Repair" for a car repair shop would be considered descriptive, while "Zenith Auto Care" would be stronger.
Likelihood of Confusion	• **Issue:** Your mark cannot be confusingly similar to an existing mark for related goods/services. Solution: Conduct a thorough search and consider the market and channels of trade. • **Example:** "Zappo's" for an online shoe store might be confusingly similar to "Zappos," but "Zappo's" for a pizza restaurant likely wouldn't be.
Genericness	• **Issue:** Generic terms can never function as trademarks. Solution: Avoid common names for products/services and create unique branding. • **Example:** "Smartphone" for a mobile phone would be generic, but "iPhone" for the same product is a strong trademark.
Failure to Police	• **Issue:** Not monitoring or enforcing your mark can lead to loss of rights. Solution: Implement a robust monitoring and enforcement strategy. • **Example:** "Aspirin" was once a trademark of Bayer but became generic in the U.S. due to lack of enforcement.

Improper Use	• **Issue:** Using your mark incorrectly can weaken its distinctiveness. Solution: Develop and follow brand usage guidelines. • **Example:** Using "Xerox" as a verb ("I'll xerox it") and as an adjective ("I'll make a Xerox copy") can weaken the mark.
Trademark Dilution	• **Issue:** Famous marks can be harmed by use that blurs or tarnishes their distinctiveness, even without confusion. Solution: For famous mark owners, actively protect against any use that could dilute your mark. • **Example:** "Kodak bicycles" could dilute the famous Kodak mark, even though there's no confusion with cameras.
Failure to Maintain Registration	• **Issue:** Not filing required maintenance documents can result in cancellation of your registration. Solution: Keep track of deadlines and file necessary documents on time. • **Example:** Forgetting to file a Section 8 Declaration between the 5th and 6th year after registration would result in cancellation.

Interactive Element

For each issue, think of an example you've encountered in real life:

1. Descriptiveness: _____

2. Likelihood of Confusion: _____

3. Genericness: _____

4. Failure to Police: _____

5. Improper Use: _____

International Trademark Considerations

Territorial Nature of Trademarks

Trademark rights are generally limited to the country of registration. This means:

- A U.S. trademark registration doesn't protect you in other countries
- Someone else could potentially use or register your mark in another country

Madrid Protocol

The Madrid Protocol allows you to file a single application to seek protection in multiple countries.

Benefits:
- Streamlined application process
- Potential cost savings for multi-country filings
- Centralized management of registrations

Considerations:
- Not all countries are members
- Vulnerable to "central attack" in the first 5 years

Paris Convention

This treaty provides a 6-month priority period to file in other member countries based on your first filing.

How it works:
1. File in your home country
2. Within 6 months, file in other member countries
3. Later applications are treated as if filed on the same day as the first application

Country-Specific Considerations

Different countries have different trademark laws and requirements. Some considerations:

1. First-to-File vs. First-to-Use Systems
- U.S. is generally first-to-use
- Many other countries are first-to-file

2. Local Use Requirements
- Some countries require proof of local use to maintain registrations

3. Language and Translation Issues
- Consider how your mark translates or transliterates in other languages

4. Classification Systems
- While many countries use the Nice Classification, there can be differences in interpretation

5. Examination Procedures
- Some countries have rigorous examination, others only check for formalities

Interactive Element

If you were expanding your business internationally, which three countries would you prioritize for trademark registration and why?

_____

_____

_____

_____

_____

_____

_____

_____

_____

Trademark Enforcement and Litigation

What Constitutes Infringement?

Trademark infringement occurs when another party uses a mark that is likely to cause confusion with your registered mark.

Factors in Determining Likelihood of Confusion

Courts consider various factors, including:

- Similarity of the marks
- Relatedness of the goods/services
- Strength of the senior mark
- Evidence of actual confusion
- Channels of trade
- Sophistication of consumers
- Defendant's intent in selecting the mark
- Likelihood of expansion of product lines

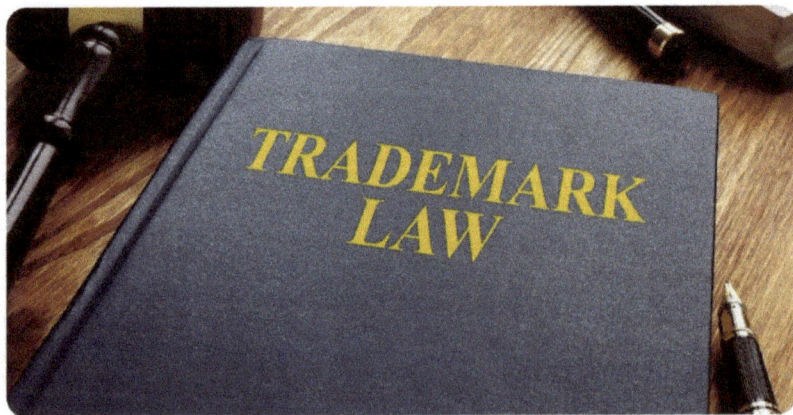

Enforcement Strategies

1.Cease and Desist Letters
- Often the first step in enforcement
- Can be an effective and cost-efficient solution

2.Negotiation and Settlement
- May involve coexistence agreements or licensing arrangements

3.TTAB Proceedings
- Opposition: Challenge a pending application
- Cancellation: Seek to cancel an existing registration

4.Federal Court Litigation
- Can seek injunctive relief and damages
- More expensive but may be necessary for serious infringement

5.Customs Recordation
- Record your registration with U.S. Customs to prevent importation of infringing goods

Remedies for Infringement

- **Injunctive Relief:** Court order to stop the infringing use
- **Monetary Damages:** Compensation for harm caused by infringement
- **Attorneys' Fees:** In exceptional cases
- **Destruction of Infringing Articles:** Court may order destruction of infringing goods

Defenses to Infringement

- Fair Use: Descriptive use of terms in good faith
- Parody: Non-commercial use for purposes of criticism or commentary
- Laches: Unreasonable delay in asserting rights
- Unclean Hands: Plaintiff's own improper conduct
- Abandonment: Discontinuation of use with intent not to resume

Interactive Element

Draft defenses that apply to your situation to discuss with your attorney.

The Future of Trademark Law

Emerging Issues in Trademark Law

1. Non-traditional Marks
- Increasing attempts to register scents, textures, holograms
- Challenges in representing and searching these marks

2. Social Media and Hashtags
- Use of trademarks in hashtags and social media handles
- Questions of infringement vs. fair use in social media contexts

3. Artificial Intelligence
- AI-generated trademarks and potential ownership issues
- Use of AI in trademark searching and enforcement

4. Virtual and Augmented Reality
- Protection of trademarks in virtual worlds
- New forms of infringement in AR/VR environments

5. Blockchain and NFTs
- Trademark issues related to blockchain domains
- Protection of trademarks in NFT marketplaces

6. International Harmonization
- Efforts to streamline trademark processes across jurisdictions
- Challenges in balancing local laws with global commerce needs

Potential Changes to Trademark Law

1. Efforts to Combat Trademark Cluttering
- Stricter use requirements to maintain registrations
- Incentives for narrower goods/services descriptions

2. Addressing Bad Faith Filings
- Increased scrutiny of applications suspected of bad faith
- Potential for new legal mechanisms to challenge bad faith registrations

3. Evolving Standards for Likelihood of Confusion
- Incorporating AI and big data in confusion analysis
- Adapting traditional factors to digital marketplace realities

4. Expansion of Anti-Dilution Protection
- Potential lowering of fame threshold for dilution claims
- Consideration of dilution in non-competing goods/services

5. Trademark Modernization Act Implementation
- New ex parte cancellation procedures
- Flexible Office Action response periods

Interactive Element

Imagine a new type of trademark that might emerge in the next 10 years.
Describe it and the challenges it might present for trademark law:

New Trademark Type: _____

Potential Challenges: _____

Interactive Exercises and Quizzes

Quiz 1: Trademark Basics

What does the ® symbol indicate?

    a) The mark is trademarked
    b) The mark is registered with the USPTO
    c) The mark is copyrighted
    d) The mark is patented

Which of the following can be trademarked?

    a) A word
    b) A logo
    c) A sound
    d) All of the above

How long does trademark registration last?

    a) 5 years
    b) 10 years
    c) 20 years
    d) Indefinitely, as long as it's renewed

What is the main purpose of conducting a trademark search?

    a) To find inspiration for new trademarks
    b) To see what your competitors are doing
    c) To avoid conflicts with existing marks
    d) To determine the cost of registration

What is trademark dilution?

    a) When a trademark becomes too common
    b) When a famous mark's distinctive quality is weakened by another's use
    c) When a trademark is used incorrectly
    d) When a trademark is not renewed on time

Quiz 1: Trademark Basics

What does the ® symbol indicate?

a) The mark is trademarked
b) The mark is registered with the USPTO
c) The mark is copyrighted
d) The mark is patented

Answer
b

Which of the following can be trademarked?

a) A word
b) A logo
c) A sound
d) All of the above

Answer
d

How long does trademark registration last?

a) 5 years
b) 10 years
c) 20 years
d) Indefinitely, as long as it's renewed

Answer
b

What is the main purpose of conducting a trademark search?

a) To find inspiration for new trademarks
b) To see what your competitors are doing
c) To avoid conflicts with existing marks
d) To determine the cost of registration

Answer
c

What is trademark dilution?

a) When a trademark becomes too common
b) When a famous mark's distinctive quality is weakened by another's use
c) When a trademark is used incorrectly
d) When a trademark is not renewed on time

Answer
b

Exercise: Create Your Own Trademark

Think of a unique product or service: _____

Create a distinctive name for it: _____

Design a simple logo (you can describe it if you can't draw):

_____
_____
_____
_____
_____
_____
_____
_____
_____
_____
_____

Write a catchy slogan:

_____

Describe how you would use this trademark in commerce:

_____

Identify potential challenges in registering this mark:

_____

Quiz 2: Advanced Trademark Concepts

What is trade dress?

  a) The clothing worn by salespeople
  b) The overall commercial image of a product
  c) A type of trademark for the fashion industry
  d) The process of designing a logo

Which of the following is NOT a factor in determining likelihood of confusion?

  a) Similarity of the marks
  b) Strength of the senior mark
  c) The trademark owner's annual revenue
  d) Evidence of actual confusion

What is the Madrid Protocol?

  a) A treaty for international patent protection
  b) A system for filing trademark applications in multiple countries
  c) A method for resolving trademark disputes
  d) A classification system for goods and services

What is genericide in trademark law?

  a) When a trademark owner kills off their brand
  b) The process of creating a new generic term
  c) When a trademark becomes the generic name for a type of product
  d) The expiration of a trademark registration

What is the purpose of a trademark watch service?

  a) To monitor for potential infringement
  b) To track the value of a trademark
  c) To provide 24/7 security for trademark certificates
  d) To time how long it takes to register a trademark

Quiz 2: Advanced Trademark Concepts

What is trade dress?

a) The clothing worn by salespeople
b) The overall commercial image of a product
c) A type of trademark for the fashion industry
d) The process of designing a logo

Answer b

Which of the following is NOT a factor in determining likelihood of confusion?

a) Similarity of the marks
b) Strength of the senior mark
c) The trademark owner's annual revenue
d) Evidence of actual confusion

Answer c

What is the Madrid Protocol?

a) A treaty for international patent protection
b) A system for filing trademark applications in multiple countries
c) A method for resolving trademark disputes
d) A classification system for goods and services

Answer b

What is genericide in trademark law?

a) When a trademark owner kills off their brand
b) The process of creating a new generic term
c) When a trademark becomes the generic name for a type of product
d) The expiration of a trademark registration

Answer c

What is the purpose of a trademark watch service?

a) To monitor for potential infringement
b) To track the value of a trademark
c) To provide 24/7 security for trademark certificates
d) To time how long it takes to register a trademark

Answer a

Glossary of Trademark Terms

- **Abandonment:** The loss of trademark rights due to discontinued use without intent to resume use.

- **Acquired Distinctiveness:** When a descriptive mark has become distinctive as a source indicator through long and exclusive use in commerce.

- **Arbitrary Mark:** A word or symbol that has a common meaning but is used to identify products or services unrelated to that meaning (e.g., "Apple" for computers).

- **Certification Mark:** A mark used to certify that products or services originate in a specific geographic region or possess certain qualities or characteristics.

- **Collective Mark:** A mark used by members of a cooperative, association, or other collective group.

- **Color Mark:** A trademark consisting solely of one or more colors used on a product or its packaging.

- **Common Law Rights:** Trademark rights acquired through use of a mark in commerce, without federal registration.

- **Concurrent Use:** When two or more parties are entitled to use the same or similar marks due to geographic separation or other factors that prevent confusion.

- **Counterfeit:** A product bearing an unauthorized reproduction of a registered trademark, intended to pass as genuine.

- **Descriptive Mark:** A mark that describes an ingredient, quality, characteristic, function, feature, purpose, or use of the specified goods or services.

- **Dilution:** The weakening of a famous trademark's distinctive quality through use of the mark by another party, even in the absence of consumer confusion.

- **Disclaimer**: A statement that the applicant or registrant does not claim exclusive rights to an unregistrable component of a mark.

- **Distinctive:** A term used to describe marks that are capable of identifying the source of goods or services.

- **Domain Name:** An internet address that may be protected as a trademark if it functions as a source identifier.

- **Examination:** The USPTO's review of a trademark application for compliance with federal law and regulations.

- **Fanciful Mark:** An invented word or symbol used as a trademark (e.g., "Kodak" for cameras).

- **Filing Basis:** The statutory basis under which a trademark application is submitted to the USPTO (e.g., use in commerce, intent to use).

- **First Use in Commerce:** The date when the mark was first used to sell goods or offer services in a type of commerce that can be regulated by the U.S. Congress.

- **Generic Term:** A word or phrase that is the common name for a type of good or service, which cannot be protected as a trademark.

- **Goods:** Products or commodities that are manufactured, produced, or sold.

- **Incontestable:** A status that may be achieved by a mark after five years on the Principal Register, providing certain legal advantages.

- **Intent-to-Use (ITU):** A basis for filing a trademark application when the applicant has a bona fide intention to use the mark in commerce but has not yet done so.

- **Likelihood of Confusion:** The primary basis for refusing registration of a trademark, occurring when a mark is likely to cause confusion with a previously registered or used mark.

- **Madrid Protocol:** An international treaty that allows a trademark owner to seek registration in any of the member countries by filing a single application.

- **Office Action:** An official letter from the USPTO explaining any legal problems with an application, including any reasons for refusal.

- **Official Gazette:** The USPTO's weekly publication where newly approved marks are published for opposition.

- **Opposition:** A proceeding in which a party seeks to prevent the registration of a published mark by filing a formal opposition with the TTAB.

- **Paris Convention:** An international treaty that provides a right of priority for trademark filings among member countries.

- **Principal Register:** The primary trademark register of the USPTO, which confers all the rights granted by the Trademark Act.

- **Priority:** The right of a party to claim a filing date earlier than the actual filing date, based on a previous application.

- **Prosecution:** The process of pursuing a trademark application at the USPTO.

- **Distinctiveness:** The ability of a mark to distinguish the source of goods or services.

- **Refusal:** The USPTO's decision not to register a mark, usually due to likelihood of confusion or descriptiveness.

- **Registration:** The official recognition and protection granted to a trademark by the USPTO.

- **Secondary Meaning**: See "Acquired Distinctiveness."

- **Section 2(f):** A provision of the Trademark Act allowing registration of descriptive marks that have acquired distinctiveness.

- **Service Mark**: A mark used to identify and distinguish the services of one provider from another.

- **Specimen:** A sample showing how the mark is actually used in commerce.

- **Stylized Mark:** A mark with a distinctive font, style, color, or design.

- **Suggestive Mark:** A mark that suggests, but does not directly describe, a quality or characteristic of the goods or services.

- **Supplemental Register:** A secondary USPTO register for marks that are not yet eligible for the Principal Register but may acquire distinctiveness in the future.

- **Surname:** A person's last name, which is not registrable as a trademark unless it has acquired distinctiveness.

- **Trade Dress:** The overall visual appearance of a product or its packaging that signifies the source of the product to consumers.

- **Trademark:** A word, phrase, symbol, design, or combination thereof that identifies and distinguishes the source of goods.

- **Trademark Trial and Appeal Board (TTAB):** The USPTO body responsible for hearing and deciding certain kinds of trademark cases, including oppositions and cancellations.

- **Use in Commerce:** The bona fide use of a mark in the ordinary course of trade.

Additional Resources

The Law Firm of Andrea Hence Evans, LLC www.evansiplaw.com

USPTO Website: www.uspto.gov
- Official source for trademark information and filings

Trademark Manual of Examining Procedure (TMEP): https://tmep.uspto.gov
- Comprehensive guide used by USPTO examiners

International Trademark Association (INTA): www.inta.org
- Global association for trademark owners and professionals

World Intellectual Property Organization (WIPO): www.wipo.int

- Updates on TTAB decisions and trademark law developments

USPTO Trademark Basics Videos:
https://www.uspto.gov/trademarks/basics/trademark-information-network

- Educational video series on various trademark topics

Trademark Status and Document Retrieval (TSDR): https://tsdr.uspto.gov

- Tool for checking the status of trademark applications and registrations

Design Search Code Manual: https://tmep.uspto.gov/RDMS/DSAM/current
- Guide for searching and coding design elements of trademarks

Trademark Fee Information: https://www.uspto.gov/trademarks/trademark-fee-information

- Current fee schedule for trademark filings and services

Remember to consult with a qualified trademark attorney for personalized advice on your specific trademark matters. The Law Firm of Andrea Hence Evans, LLC is standing by to help you with your patent, trademark and copyright legal matters.

THE LAW FIRM OF
ANDREA HENCE EVANS
PATENT • TRADEMARK • COPYRIGHT

INVEST IN YOUR IDEA®

About The Law Firm of Andrea Hence Evans, LLC

The Law Firm of Andrea Hence Evans, LLC, specializes in providing comprehensive intellectual property services, including patent, trademark, and copyright law. Founded by Andrea Hence Evans, Esq., the firm leverages her extensive expertise gained during her tenure at the United States Patent and Trademark Office (USPTO), where she served as both a Patent Examiner and a Trademark Examining Attorney.

With a commitment to empowering innovators and businesses, the firm guides clients through the complex processes of securing and protecting their intellectual property. Known for its tailored, client-focused approach, the firm has successfully represented inventors, entrepreneurs, and organizations, ensuring their creative ideas and brand assets are legally safeguarded.

About Andrea Hence Evans, Esq.

Andrea Hence Evans, Esq., is a trailblazing attorney whose unique career path began at the USPTO. A graduate of The George Washington University Law School, Andrea's legal acumen is complemented by her engineering background from Georgia Tech and Spelman College. Her dual expertise in law and science equips her with the insights needed to navigate the technical and legal intricacies of intellectual property cases.

During her tenure at the USPTO, Andrea evaluated patent applications across mechanical and electrical fields and conducted comprehensive trademark examinations. Her in-depth knowledge of USPTO procedures and policies makes her a sought-after advocate for those seeking to protect their inventions and brands.

Andrea's accolades include recognition as a White House STEM Champion of Change and the Nation's Best Advocate: 40 Lawyers Under 40 by the National Bar Association. Beyond her professional achievements, she is dedicated to educating the community about intellectual property rights, frequently serving as a speaker and thought leader in her field.

At The Law Firm of Andrea Hence Evans, LLC, Andrea and her team are committed to helping clients turn their innovative ideas into legally protected assets, ensuring their intellectual property receives the recognition and protection it deserves.

Office: (301) 497-9997

info@evansiplaw.com

14625 Baltimore Ave. #853
Laurel, MD 20707

www.evansiplaw.com

@evansiplaw